If Heart Could Speak

Deepali Agrawal

BookLeaf Publishing

India | USA | UK

Presentation by *BookLeaf Publishing*

Web: www.bookleafpub.com

E-mail: info@bookleafpub.com

ISBN: 9789358313703

First edition 2023

*I dedicate my book to my lovely children
whose love is beyond my imagination:
KDAKLA*

*My angel in heaven my heartbeat : Dad
thanks to your blessings on me that my
second book is out as well. I Love You.*

ACKNOWLEDGEMENT

My sister my bestie my world, no day or night is completed without you. My mentor, my bestie, my guide, my punching pillow and my to go person I Love You lots.

My husband thanks for the unspoken support and love you give me which became my strength to write more.

My mother for all the life lessons and encouragement and immense love.

My partner (Manu) you are the best jijs I could have asked for.

My friends and family who gave me so much love and support that my second book got published. Not possible without you.

PREFACE

If Heart Could Speak, the world will be a better place to live. People, life, relationships would be much better defined and hatred would be empowered by emotions. A friend talking endlessly, or a pregnant mom speaking to her unborn child, baby saying I love you would be so easily expressed if only heart could speak. Through the median of my second book let's experience the journey of an unspoken heart in a more deeper and refined way. Life is short and unexpected so get out of the shell through reading thee poems and give your heart a chance to speak out loud as it can.

Love

Gentle touch and whispered sighs,
Love paints the world mesmerizing skies.
Every glimpse with a tender silent kiss,
Resides a satisfaction of endless bliss.
Surpassing trials and storms endured,
Love shines bright and eternity assured.
Poet's beautiful creation like a melodious song,
Love is a combination of sweet yet bond so strong.
In love we find God's deepest faith,
Pure as gold not complicated but straight.

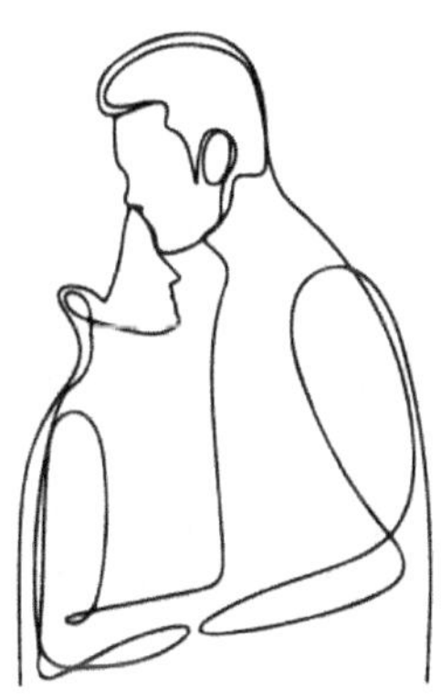

Sunrise

As the dawn breaks it silence,
A canvas once so dark awaits its solace.
Slicing through the darkness ready to give world
a new homage,
Painting the whole sky with crimson red and
orange.
Birds takes a flight with melodious song,
Welcoming the day with open arms for lifelong.
Each dawn brings forth a splendid sight,
A symphony of colors, rejoice pure and bright.
A promise of new dreams and rebirth,
Sunrise the herald of the Earth.

Stranger

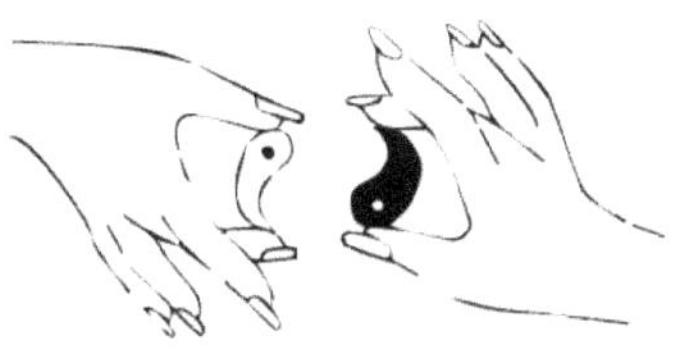

In the world so crowded so many faces we pass,
Some are frosty others clear as a glass.
Some walk with purpose others lost in thought,
A myriad of stories, silently wrought.
Each novel yet to be read,
A universe of thoughts in each head.
Eyes full of mysteries stories untold,
Journeys they have travelled yet to unfold.
Smiles exchanged a sweet connection awaits,
Might be a simple pass or a lifelong friendship
written in the fate.
Each one a wonder, a mystery unknown,
In this beautiful world of strangers , we're never
alone.

Angel

A presence is felt within so deep,
Giving a sense of warmth not a reason to weep.
A sense of confidence is felt,
Any battle of good or evil is dealt.
A blessing in disguise left too soon,
Far above in sky he lives like a boon.
Tired of walking through stress in pain I sing,
My Angel arrives in a blink to carry me afloat
on his wings.

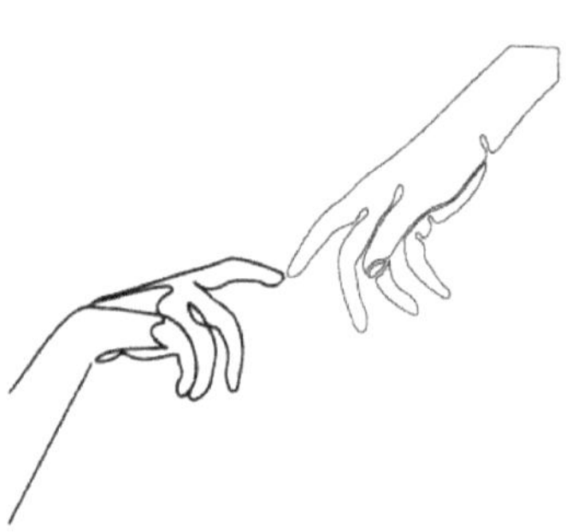

Broken Smile

A smile once so happy and gay seems to lost its
way,
In a cracked joy it fades to gray.
The cracks reveals a hidden treasure,
A smile once so bright has forgotten the way to
true pleasure.
Behind the crack lies tales untold,
A journey marked soul so bold.
Bend in the smile yet still it grins,
A battle to win a new story to begin.
Though broken yet not shattered,
Beautiful colored feather yet again gathered.
For in that smile so worn an torn,
Resides a million hopes to be reborn.

Memories

In the corner of my heart lies a chest,
Filled with memories of my life from past lived
the best.
A series of joy and tears,
Moments held across the years.
Each fragment like a melodious song,
Where echoes of our past years belong.
The twinkle in an old friend's eyes,
A childhood love that makes us sigh.
The scent that engulfs the air,
A short memory of a love affair.
Memories are the best threads that bind,
A knitting of the heart, soul and mind.
Through them we feel the warmth of the days
long gone,
In every note of life's sweet melodious song.

Dreams

In the silence of the night where fantasies take
flight,
Invisible worlds painting the dark night.
A place where wishes bloom and hope takes
form,
In our palace where we are reborn.
With closed eyes we dare to fly a far,
To chase and touch the most distant star.
Dreams are the canvas where souls are free,
Unchained by reality we become what we see.
Whispers of the heart's secret desire,
A war where imagination set the world on fire.
When the morning light tears through the
blissful night,
A gorgeous new dawn gives us the strength to
fight.

To carry on the dreams we wove all night in
sheer,
To make our wishes real by bridging the world
here and there.

Sip of Coffee

In the silent dawn's gentle touch,
A steam potion of aroma means so much.
From a bean to deep sip is a journey traced,
A warn hug in a mug tightly embraced.
Dark depths brewed in the morning light,
The only way to banish the long night.
Its warmth is an embrace to hold,
Every sip has million stories to unfold.
It ignites a conversation and fuel to the mind,
A forever companion one of its kind.
Beginning of a journey at its start,
Coffee, the aroma that fills your heart.

Son

In the cradle of love, a precious little one arrives,
Future dreams a true joy of parents lives.
Tiny cute giggles to hearty laugh,
Tall as he stands besides us so tough.
As his journey unfolds a dream yo weave,
With each step his ambitions he'll achieve.
From boy hood to manhood grace,
He has a journey of his own to embrace.
In his heart courage and compassion blend,
A son, a joy , God send a lifetime friend.

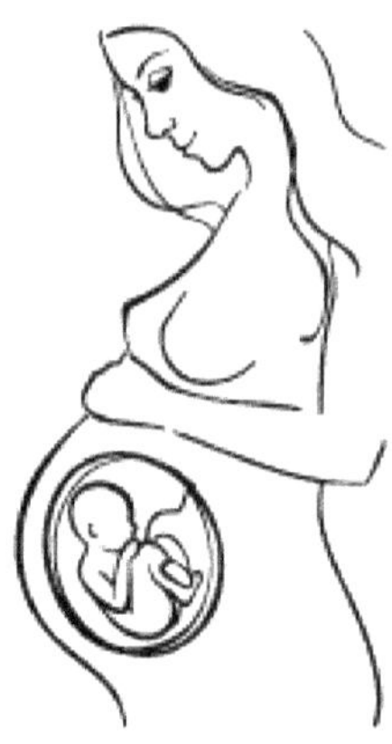

Whisper

In a hush of a mother's soft voice,
Lies a lullaby sung as a blessing in disguise.
Soft words that dance on fleeting air,
Carrying lifelong secrets, love and care.
In youth they flutter like leaves in gentle breeze,
Whispers, a messenger of mysteries.
A murmur shared, a secret exchanged,
With a gentle touch a trust arranged.
In the gentle breeze of air,
A calming touch of love a hope delivered in
middle of despair.

Sisters

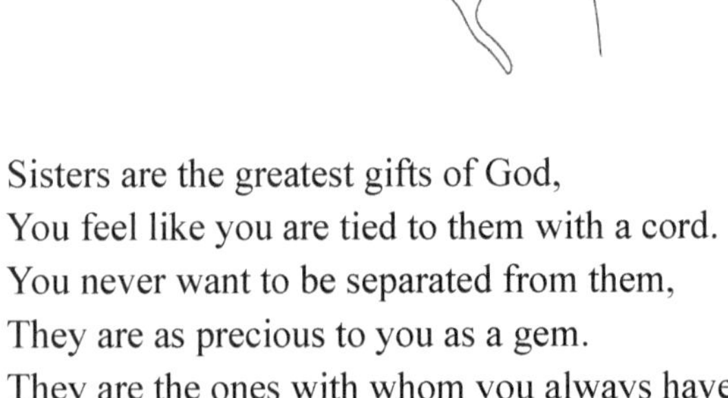

Sisters are the greatest gifts of God,
You feel like you are tied to them with a cord.
You never want to be separated from them,
They are as precious to you as a gem.
They are the ones with whom you always have fights,
But you still love them to the heights.
In good as well as bad times they are always there by you,
Sisters are the one who guide you in whatever you do.
They are the ones you can confide in,
They help you to distinguish between virtue and sin.
If they see you loose, they also push you to win,
You are the fish and they are tour fins.

They make you laugh and they make you cry,
They make you shine like a star in the night sky.
You are the apple of their eye,
To sisters its very tough to say a good bye.
At the end of the day one must thank the lord,
As sisters are one of the best blessings of GOD.

Soul

Inside us a spark do reside,
A flame so eternal and bright deep inside.
A true essence of truly who we are,
Shining light from within our forever star.
Soul. silent whisper of the heart,
Divine God's most beautiful eternal piece of art.
Untouched by the cruel touch of life,
So pure immortal untouched by any sharp knife.
Through good or bad it remains constant,
Your true forever companion from present to
past.
It yearns for love, growth and connection,
A self satisfaction, a strong inner reflection.
In moment of doubts it offers solace,
A constant reminder of our inner peace.
A mere traveller from one body to another,

Carrier for our desire, our dreams from one
world to other.
So cherish your soul, let it be your guide,
in its solace let your peaceful mind reside.

Journey of Spirituality

Embarking on a journey of spirituality,
Mysteries unfold through awakening our minds
to reality.
A path of discovery, where wisdom unfolds,
Through valley of doubts, and alley of fears,
Our spiritual Guru through his knowledge makes
our mind clear.
 In silence and stillness with constant chanting,
Our soul finds the way it's been wanting.
Through meditation and connection we find our
way,
Connecting with true self helping not to be
astray.
We learn to let go, surrender ourselves,
With full trust we let our soul from any doubt
resolve.

For in this exploration, we find our true selves,
Connected to something greater, where divinity
dwells.
For in the depths of spirituality's embrace,
We find peace, love, and infinite grace.

Beauty

In this world, beauty do reside,
In every corner it cannot hide.
It is in the blooming flower so mesmerizing and
bright,
In the golden sunrise shining so vibrant.
Beauty lies in an innocent smile,
Little acts of kindness goes an extra mile.
In a child's laughter that fills the air,
Or just a gentle touch to show we care.
Beauty lies in the melody of a bird's song,
Or how our body wishes to sway along.
Beauty lies in form of your mother's blessing
hand,
Or those loud cheering your father makes
winning strand.
Beauty is not just what we see,

But flying in the moments that sets us free.
So embrace this little moments of beauty
everyday,
As in these lies the secrets to rejoice in the
simplest way.

Forever Love

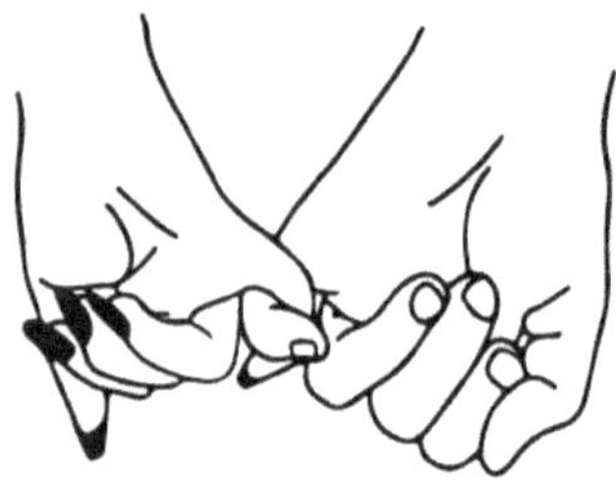

In the depth of my soul a flame burns,
A love so pure and warm it"s hard to discern.
It gives a warm fuzzy feeling deep inside,
A sense of immense security in me resides.
True love like a shining light guiding me in dark
night,
Those moment of ease and making gray days
bright.
It needs no rules or limit or bound,
Deep inside the heart like a sweet symphony
sound.
With every heart beat my heart your name sings,
In the midst of silence like a melody it rings.
In your eyes i see my forever,
A bond , a promise , a love which would not
leave us ever.

Together hand in hand we will journey together side by side,
Our trust and promise will makes us surf through any tide.

Reflection

In the silence of moment I find myself thinking,
A true reflection of my past yet the battle is debating.
Thoughts flow like ripples in silent lake,
Reflects, ponder my emotions to be awake.
I ponder on the paths I once walked,
Decisions made , broken promises and lies talked.
Regrets and triumphs intertwined,
Lessons learned and wisdom redefined.
Through the highs and lows I thought,
Good or bad were my own battles fought.
In moments of silence, I find clarity,
A deeper understanding of my own identity.
To cherish the present, let go of the past,
Embrace the future, for it comes fast.
I look at myself in the mirror with affection,
In this journey of better me, I accept with love and grace my real reflection.

Long Distance

It is not easy loving someone from a distance
moreover,
But the pain of being so far draws the love
closer.
The longing to see the one I love reaffirms in my
heart,
That the love is for real it wont run away like the
tide putting you in the dirt.
It wont fade away like a distant landscape,
It will become what we have been waiting
patiently for-
A relationship that's not distant.
A relationship that's so strong.
A relationship that's so pure.
A relationship that's going to reach beyond
eternity for sure.

Happiness

Happiness is not a distant dream,
But a gleam of light in our best reflected shining beam.
It dances in our heart like a gentle breeze,
Giving our mind and soul it's peaceful ease.
Happiness resides in smile of a child,
Or in a hearty laughter with your friends so wild.
It dwells in the beauty of a morning dew,
Warm silent hug in bed for start of the day in minutes or few.
Happiness lies in the warm tight friendship embrace,
Love and bond of a family in a safe secure space.
It's not a destination, but a melodious journey we create,
Filled with affirmations or positive vibes we generate.

For happiness lies in our heart,
Cherish and respect the most beautiful God's
work of art.

Slow

Lives lost and lessons learnt,
Family and loved ones come around first.
Laugh and talk a little together,
Create lovely memories forever.
This time will come back or not,
Moments spend around with much deeper
thought.
Inhaling the beauty of nature,
Creating a much better example for a better
future.
Take a deep breath and walk a little slow,
Smile a lot and worry less to make your
memories which would shine and glow.

Dad

I have to admit that I was daddy's girl,
He told me he loved me better than anything else
in the world.
My trophy, my first walk on the aisle,
He gave me away with a bittersweet teary smile.
When I gave birth,
He was there too to greet my little one and say I
love you too.
The man who wrapped me so strong and tight in
his arms,
He has gone on his own journey to a forever sky
so warm.
Far away from my touch not to be seen,
The love which he left is so strong and powerful.
I'll keep his memory and legacy alive and honor
all that he believed,
And forever grateful for all his love that i
received.